DESIGNER DRUGS

Drug problems affect many young people in our society.

THE DRUG ABUSE PREVENTION LIBRARY

DESIGNER DRUGS

Lawrence Clayton, Ph.D.

THE ROSEN PUBLISHING GROUP, INC.
NEW YORK

To those addicts who were closest to me:
My dad - "Big Keith,"
My uncle - Jim,
My brother - "Little Keith,"
Who all died prematurely from their addictions.

The people pictured in this book are only models; they, in no way, practice or endorse the activities illustrated. Captions serve only to explain the subjects of the photographs and do not imply a connection between real-life models and the staged situations shown. News agency photographs are exceptions.

Published in 1994 by The Rosen Publishing Group, Inc.
29 East 21st Street, New York, NY 10010

First Edition

Manufactured in the United States of America

Cover: An assortment of screw caps and other items found by police in a drug raid.

Library of Congress Cataloging-in-Publication Data

Clayton, L. (Lawrence)
      Designer drugs/by Lawrence O. Clayton—1st ed.,
      p.   cm.—(The Drug abuse prevention library)
      Includes bibliographical references and index.
          ISBN 0-8239-1519-0
          1. Drug abuse—United States—Juvenile
      literature. 2. Designer drugs—United States—
      Juvenile literature.   I. Title.   II. Series.
      HV5825.C575   1994   93-23497
      362.29'9'0973—dc20   CIP
                                   AC

Contents

Introduction   *6*

Chapter 1   What Are Designer Drugs?   *9*

Chapter 2   How Do You Get Them?   *15*

Chapter 3   What Kinds Are There?   *25*

Chapter 4   Why People Use Drugs   *49*

Chapter 5   Where to Get Help   *53*

Help List   *60*

Glossary—*Explaining New Words*   *61*

For Further Reading   *62*

Index   *63*

Introduction

A new and unexpected danger is lurking in our neighborhoods. It has destroyed more lives than anything we've seen before. That danger is designer drugs.

Police have tried to stop the danger. Former President Ronald Reagan declared war on it. He used Navy and Coast Guard ships, Air Force planes, and Army helicopters to fight it. Parents have warned their kids. Pastors and rabbis have preached against it. School systems have tried to control it. Nothing has worked.

Designer drugs are more easily available than ever. Elementary school children are using them. Adolescents are using them. There is hardly a team, school, factory, club, or church youth group in which designer drugs have not made an impact.

Wives have left their husbands, husbands have left their wives, parents have abandoned their children. Workers have quit their jobs. Police have turned to crime. All because of designer drugs.

What are these designer drugs? How have they managed to create such terrible trouble in our society? Where do they come from? What do they do? Those questions, and many more, are answered in this book. It is important for you to read it. It could save your life or the life of someone you love.

If you think you or a friend have been exposed to a designer drug, get help immediately. Read Chapter 5 to discover your options.

Tell your family, friends, teacher, minister, priest, or rabbi about this book. The more people who know, the more lives could be saved.

Getting involved with drugs causes many serious problems.

CHAPTER 1

What Are Designer Drugs?

*D*esigner drugs are synthetic. They are usually made in illegal laboratories by chemists or "cooks" who have little or no laboratory training or experience. Only a few of the cooks really know what they are doing.

The laboratories (also called "labs," "crack houses," or "cook joints") are often dirty, smelly, and full of things that get into the drugs being made. Police have found moldy bread, rotting food, sewage, garbage, bloody instruments, and even dead animals and human bodies in these laboratories. The cooks are often drug addicts themselves. They may be stoned, high, or drunk.

10   It costs a lot of money to set up laboratories. Usually they are financed by "businessmen" who want to make a lot of money fast. They don't care about you, your family, or your friends. All they care about is the money. They buy the cheapest equipment and the cheapest chemicals, and they hire the least expensive cook they can find. If a few people die, go insane, or are left permanently crippled, who cares? They've done what they set out to do— make a lot of money.

These laboratories have no quality control as do companies that make drugs you buy in the drugstore. That makes the synthetic drugs very dangerous. Just cooking a batch of drugs over a little higher heat or a bit longer turns it into deadly poison. Addicts have been found dead with the needle still in their arm.

The drugs these labs make are extremely dangerous. They have resulted in untold thousands of deaths. Thousands more users have been crippled. The physical problems they cause include heart attack, stroke, lung disease, eye problems, paralysis, Parkinson's-like symptoms (the shakes), stomach problems, unconsciousness, nosebleeds, insomnia (inability to sleep), nausea, vomiting (sometimes for hours), spitting up blood, and destruction of brain cells.

The mental problems they cause include paranoia, severe depression, psychosis (insanity), anxiety, aggression (sometimes so severe that the user kills an innocent bystander), anhedonia (inability to experience pleasure of any kind), and extreme social withdrawal (resulting in the loss of those most loved).

A designer drug is usually much more powerful than the drug it is designed to replace. One particular designer drug is so powerful that a single dose is smaller than a single grain of sugar—and two grains could kill you.

Almost all drugs are cut (have other substances added) to increase the amount that can be sold. Designer drugs are usually cut with the same substance as the drug they were designed to replace. For that reason few drug users can tell the difference between them. People often use them not knowing that they are using a designer drug.

When a few grains of a powerful designer drug are mixed into a large amount of cut, it is easy to make a mistake. The smallest mistake can produce a dose that will kill the user.

12

Phil and Gene were brothers, the only children of a poor Los Angeles family. They both quit school to support their parents.

Their mother was dying of cancer. Their father had had a stroke. He had managed to live at home where his wife took care of him. But then his health began to worsen. The brothers were very worried.

On the way home from work they stopped to buy some China White. Their mother found Phil in the bathroom later, the needle still in his arm. She rushed outside to get Gene to help. She found him slumped over the steering wheel of his car. He too was dead, a needle in his arm.

Why did these brothers die? Because a cook had turned up the stove just a few degrees to hurry the product along. He had created a deadly poison instead of China White.

A young couple, Rick and Martina, were on their honeymoon. A friend had turned them on to angel dust, a designer drug that often causes paranoia in users.

Late one evening, Rick took a dose. Shortly afterward he began hallucinating (seeing things that weren't there), and he became paranoid. He screamed over and over again, "Stay away from me! Don't touch me!" Martina couldn't calm him down, so she called the police.

When the police arrived, Rick beat them up. He kicked in the door of the next room, and the guest shot him in the chest. Even after Rick had lost a lot of blood, it took six policemen to subdue him.

A 12-year-old girl and her 14-year-old boyfriend had never used drugs before. The girl's older brother convinced them that a little crack wouldn't hurt them.

They started doing crack that evening and spent all their money within an hour.

The girl then traded sex to several of her brother's friends for more crack. It was her first experience with sex.

Her parents returned home to find their daughter having sex in front of six teenage boys. They also found their son in the kitchen doing crack.

What could cause such tragedies? How could a drug be so powerful as to make people do things that they normally would never do?

Designer drugs have done that and much, much more! Read on to discover how you can protect yourself from them.

Drugs are often available through a network of friends.

CHAPTER 2

How Do You Get Them?

*T*he answer to that question is, "Almost anywhere." It is unfortunate, but true. No place is truly drug-free these days. We get drugs from friends, peers, family members, other adults, and dealers.

Friends sometimes do drugs. If they do, sooner or later they will offer them to you. Often they believe they are doing you a favor by including you in what they do.

Daniel, 14, had a good friend named John. They were the same age, in the same classes, and liked the same things. They seemed closer than brothers.

John had started smoking crack a few months ago. He had told Daniel. Now he

genetics

16 *offered him some of the drug. Daniel knew how much John liked crack. He felt honored that John would share it with him. But should he take it?*

It is no surprise that one of the biggest sources of drugs is a person's own family. That is because drug use runs in families. People who become addicted are born with a *genetic code* that makes addiction much more likely.

The brain contains a chemical called endorphin. It gives us a feeling of well-being. It is released after we exercise, when our team wins, or when a member of the opposite sex thinks we are cute.

When most of us use a drug, our body breaks it down into substances that it uses, stores, or expels. But when people who have the genetic code use a drug, their body turns part of it into THIQ, a suppressor chemical. What it suppresses is endorphin. When endorphin is not active, drug users are not able to feel good until they use more of the drug.

Family members have similar genetic codes. That means that if one of you is addicted, the rest of the family is at risk. If you start using, you will quickly become addicted.

Drug addiction can become costly and ruin a person's ability to lead a constructive and successful life.

18

Susie was Paul's older sister. She and Paul had always been close. Their parents both drank a lot, and Paul and Susie were often at home alone. When Paul was younger, Susie took care of him.

Now that Susie had her own apartment, Paul visited her often. Sometimes he spent the night. It was better than being at home alone. In the morning Susie would cook breakfast for him and drop him off at school on her way to work.

One weekend he caught a ride to her apartment. He knew she was having a party because of all the cars outside and the loud music. When he walked in, someone handed him a beer. Susie came and introduced him around. Later someone handed him a marijuana cigarette. Paul thought it was cool.

What Paul didn't know was that both his father and his mother had the genetic code for addiction. He had it, too. He had just begun the long process of ending up a junkie. It was only a matter of time before drugs would be a serious problem for him.

Peers often get other kids to sample drugs. In some schools and communities almost everyone uses them. It's the "in" thing to do.

Amy had been going to a new school for **19**
about a month. The kids seemed friendly
enough but a little distant. Jill, a girl Amy
hardly knew, asked her if she wanted to
"hang out" after school. They were all going
to a local hamburger joint. "Yes!" said Amy,
right away. She was excited about finally
being included.

After school she walked to the hamburger
joint. All the other girls were sitting in or
standing around cars. Jill said, "Hi, Amy;
boy, do we have some bad stuff here." Then
she handed her a pipe.

"What is this?" asked Amy. "It's cool,"
said Jill, "go ahead." "Yeah!" said the others,
"go ahead." Amy answered, "No, thanks."
She handed the pipe back to Jill and walked
away. She thought, "It's going to be a long
year."

That is peer pressure. It is hard to
handle. What would you do if you were in
Amy's place? Would you use the drug? Or
would you walk away? Could you have
done that?

Dealers are another source of drugs—
obviously the major one. Most of the
illegal drugs in this country come through
dealers. Dealers make their living by selling drugs.

There are many ways to have a good time without drugs.

Designer drugs are sold to dealers. The dealers cut the drug by mixing in other substances. Then they sell the mixture to other dealers. Each dealer cuts it in turn. That happens many times.

Dealers want to sell their drug as quickly as possible. They also want to make as much money as they can.

Carlos knew that Zana was a dealer. Everybody knew it. Zana was always hanging around. People came up to him and handed him money. They left with drugs.

Zana often stared at Carlos. He would stare, then throw back his head and laugh. Only it didn't sound like a laugh. It sounded mean. Carlos was afraid of Zana.

Sometimes Zana would yell at Carlos. "Boy," he would say, "I got your stuff here. You know you want it. You're going to do it. Why not now?" Carlos would run home. And Zana would laugh.

Carlos had seen what happened to people. First they bought Zana's drugs. Then they quit going to school. Finally they were no good at all.

But everyone looked up to Zana. He always had money and pretty girls. He had a great car. Carlos wished he had Zana's car. But he never wanted Zana's drugs.

22

One day Zana said, "Hey, Carlos, I'll give you five dollars to take this to Shena." Carlos ran to Shena's house and gave her the package. That was the beginning. Soon he was delivering packages all over the neighborhood.

Then one day Zana was smoking some stuff. "Take a hit," said Zana, "you a man or a wimp?" Carlos took the cigarette and inhaled the smoke. His lungs burned, and he started coughing. Zana laughed. "I'll have to start you on something easy."

Later, Zana gave Carlos a pill. "Take this," he said. Within a month, Carlos was using drugs regularly. Now, when he delivers packages, he gets half his pay in drugs.

Dealers often act as if they are your friend. Some of them will give you free samples so you will get hooked. Dealers are no one's friend.

Crack is known by many street names. Among them are gravel, Roxanne, base, baseball, rock, people, and super coke.

Moon rock is a mixture of crack and heroin. Its purpose is to help the addict come down off a crack high without the terrible depression. What happens is that the user ends up with two addictions, one for crack and one for heroin.

Crack use brings many problems: **23**

- Instant and severe addiction.
- A life of crime.
- Birth defects in children.
- Antisocial behavior. Addicts don't care about anything except the drug.
- Physical symptoms such as stroke, nausea and vomiting, lung problems, and nosebleeds. Permanent lung damage may occur.
- Psychological problems such as depression, sleeplessness, anhedonia (inability to experience pleasure), and schizophrenia (a loss of touch with reality).

Some drugs distort reality and affect your ability to perceive
situations properly.

CHAPTER 3

What Kinds Are There?

*I*n this chapter we take a closer look at each of the designer drugs. We'll discover its history, and especially what drug it was designed to replace. We'll find out if it has a medical purpose. We'll learn the street names of each drug, what it looks like, how it is used, and what effect it has.

We will also look at the damage each drug does to the user. This is important because each drug damages its user in a different way.

Ecstasy

Peyote is a drug that was used by the Yaqui Indians in Mexico and the south-western United States. Peyote comes from

26 the cactus plant. It was used by some Native Americans in religious ceremonies.

Peyote is a *psychedelic* drug. That means that it makes the user hear and see things that aren't there. Moving things seem to have a "tail" like a comet. Even a moving hand or a car has a tail. The user may also see double. At other times, things appear to vibrate.

Ecstasy is a laboratory-made drug designed to act like peyote. It is more expensive than most of the designer drugs. It costs $30 to $50 per dose.

People call Ecstasy by several names: X, XTC, X-ray, Adam, Lovebug, or the "love" drug. It gets the last two nicknames because of an effect it has on the user. Instead of feeling a "rush," the user feels loving and close to other people. Users often cry and hug persons around them.

In the past, Ecstasy was sold under the chemical name MDMA. It was used by psychologists to help people who were withdrawn. In some cases, it actually seemed to work.

When the illegal laboratories began to make it, they cut it with other substances. They did this to increase the amount of drug so they could get more money. Each dealer cut the product until it was only one tenth Ecstasy and nine tenths cut. Dealers and addicts call this "stepping on" the drug.

Some of the most common cuts used in Ecstasy are caffeine, amphetamine (an addictive drug known as "speed"), baking soda, and several kinds of sugar.

Among the side effects of Ecstasy use are nausea and vomiting—sometimes for hours. Users have been known to drown in their own vomit. Like peyote users, they also see tails on objects, see objects vibrate, and have double vision. In addition, they get the shakes, sweat profusely, and become disoriented.

Ecstasy causes rapid changes in blood pressure and heart rate. Some users have died from heart attack and stroke. Users report not feeling physical pain. Many users clench their jaws so hard that they break teeth and bite their cheeks.

The high from Ecstasy may last up to six hours. But the user is likely to be exhausted for days afterward.

The psychological effects of the drug are varied. Some users report feeling close to others and being able to work through relationship problems. Others report feeling paranoid, extremely anxious, numb, and depressed for days after use.

28 This drug, like all drugs, affects the way the brain works. It destroys many normal brain chemicals. Some never replace themselves.

If you see this drug, it will probably be in pill form—usually white, tan, or brown. It is sometimes made in capsules, but those are rare and very expensive.

Crack

Cocaine is a drug made from the coca plant. It is found in the mountains of South America. It helps the Indians work high in the mountains without pain. As they carry supplies up the steep trails, they chew the leaves.

The Indians are very healthy, and the coca leaves help them to stay that way. The coca provides vitamin C, thiamine, and riboflavin. In some ways, one could compare the Indians' use of the coca leaf to our use of aspirin as a pain reliever.

Not so with the drug cocaine. It is a dangerous drug that is very addictive and has caused many deaths.

Most of the people who use cocaine either *snort* it or smoke it. To snort it they usually spread it on a mirror. Then they use a razor blade to chop it up and form the powder into lines. They use a small

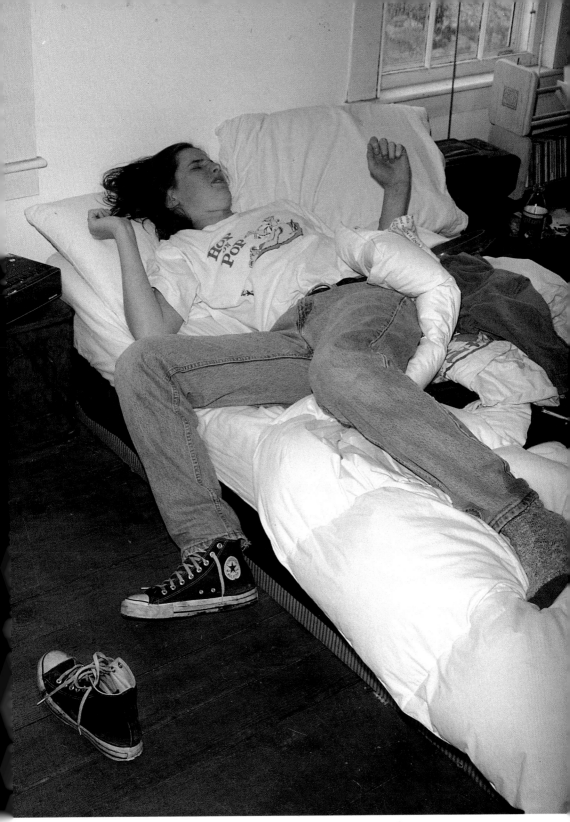

Instead of producing a "good high," drugs often create feelings of depression and discomfort.

30 straw or a rolled-up dollar bill to inhale the drug. That is how cocaine got one of its street names—nose candy.

Cocaine can also be *mainlined*. This means injecting the drug into a vein with a needle. The rush from mainlining is an intense feeling of well-being, peacefulness, and bursts of energy and power. It is much more intense than from snorting. The effect is experienced instantly.

Drug users know exactly how to get the high they want.

Some people smoke cocaine. They use a pipe shaped like a ball on the bottom, with a neck. To do this in the most effective way, cocaine must be *freebased*. Freebasing cocaine is a process of cooking the drug and inhaling the vapor. In this form the drug gives a more powerful rush.

One of the dangers of freebased cocaine is that it is very explosive. Many people have been injured. Some have been burned beyond recognition.

Crack is really nothing more than cocaine that has been prepared to be freebased. It forms small clumps of a claylike substance. This hardens into "rock cocaine" or crack.

Many people think that crack is pure because it gives such a powerful rush. It is no more pure than cocaine. It has been cut with all the same things. Remember, before crack was cooked, it *was* cocaine. It may have been cut with sugar, caffeine, a laxative, speed, talcum powder, or any number of other substances.

The rush from smoking crack is extremely intense. But it does not last long (maybe as long as 10 minutes). The smoke goes directly to the lungs, where it is absorbed. This process sends the drug straight to the brain. It is the most direct

Drug-addicted teens often steal money from family members to support their habit.

route. After the rush wears off, the user suffers an equally extreme and intense depression. That leaves the user craving more crack.

This process is so powerful that many persons become hopelessly addicted after just one episode. After that, they will do almost anything to get more. They will steal, sell their bodies for sex, even kill.

While this is obviously very bad for the user, it is very good for the dealer's business. Dealers love to get people hooked on crack. They know that addicts will buy more and more of the drug. Cocaine users may quit doing drugs for a time. Crack users seldom quit. Because of this, it has become a $100 billion business.

The usual price for a dose of crack is about $25. However, it is so addictive that some people develop a $4,000-dollar-a-month habit. That's around 160 "hits" (doses) a month.

A crack house is where users can go to use the drug. They usually stay for days at a time, using one dose after another until their money runs out. At that point, the females begin trading sex for drugs. The males may leave to pawn their belongings or to steal. When they have enough to buy more crack, they usually return.

China White

The drug morphine was used as a pain-killer in the last century. During the Civil War many soldiers became addicted to morphine. This terrible problem ended up killing many of them and ruining the lives of others.

Heroin was developed to break morphine addiction. People thought heroin was not addictive. It seemed to be the answer to the problems that morphine addiction created. It was considered a "hero" drug. That is how it came to be called heroin.

As it turned out, heroin was much more addictive than morphine. In fact, more people became addicted to it than were addicted to morphine. Worldwide, only alcohol is more addictive.

Among the effects of heroin, users feel a higher tolerance for pain, frequently "nod off" (fall asleep), lose their motivation, suffer a lack of energy, have an "I don't care" attitude, and lack interest in food. Heroin is a "downer," and downers cause a lack of interest in everything.

There are about 500,000 heroin addicts in the United States. Thousands of people die from heroin use each year. It is a major problem.

Federal, national, state, and local police **35** are doing everything possible to stop people from bringing heroin into this country. Because of that, drug dealers and users have been looking for something to replace it. In the late 1970s, they found it.

Illegal laboratories began to manufacture a substance that came to be called China White. (Street heroin usually comes in a white powdery form.)

Homemade and illegal labs produce various designer drugs.

36

China White is *more* dangerous than heroin. There are several reasons for that.

- It is 175 to 6,000 times more powerful than morphine.
- There is no way to control the quality as it is made in illegal laboratories.
- It has to be cut. It has been cut with almost every white powder, from lactose (milk sugar) or fructose (fruit sugar), to mannitol (a laxative), and strychnine (a deadly poison). It may also be cut with caramel or brown dye (to make it look like "China Brown"—a cheaper brown heroin).
- Very little of the drug is needed to get stoned. Four grains can be fatal.
- It is often mixed with heroin. Some people can take a lot of heroin. NO ONE can take a lot of China White.
- If it is cooked too hot, it turns into MPTP, a poison so lethal that victims usually die with the needle still in their arm.

The chemical name for China White is *fentanyl*. Several other drugs are closely related to fentanyl.

Most people cannot tell the difference between these drugs and heroin. Because of that, many thousands have suffered permanent damage, or death.

How Is It Used?

China White is used like heroin. People mainline it, "lace" (put it on) cigarettes and smoke it, or snort it. It can also be "skin-popped"—injected under the skin. This gives a more intense rush than snorting the drug, but not as intense as mainlining it. Most users go from smoking to snorting, to skin-popping, to mainlining. Each step gives a more powerful rush.

Why Do People Use It?

People use China White for several reasons. The usual reason is for the rush. For a brief period users feel wonderful, and all their problems seem to vanish.

Most people who use China White think they are using heroin. Their dealer, or someone the dealer got the drug from, mixed in China White.

Some people use the drug knowing that it is China White. They do so because it is cheaper than heroin.

Most people use China White because they are "hooked," or addicted to the drug. Heroin is extremely addictive. Once they start using, it is very difficult to stop.

The rush people get from China White is much shorter than the one from heroin. So they have to use it again to avoid the pain of withdrawal.

China White is made in illegal laboratories in the United States. It isn't smuggled in from Asia like heroin. Therefore it is much more easily available than heroin.

People use drugs to overcome personal problems. In the end, they have all the problems they had in the beginning. They also have a whole new set of problems. They are criminals, and they are addicted to a very powerful drug.

What Problems Does It Cause?
China White is dangerous. Police can tell whenever a new laboratory starts making it. That is because of the dead bodies of users they find. It is also because of the huge numbers of users who show up in hospital emergency rooms.

This drug causes numerous physical problems:

- China White is very addictive. Almost everyone who uses it ends up hooked. This is called *high addictive potential*.
- Addicts can usually tell when they have injected China White because of the *burning-arm syndrome*. The arm

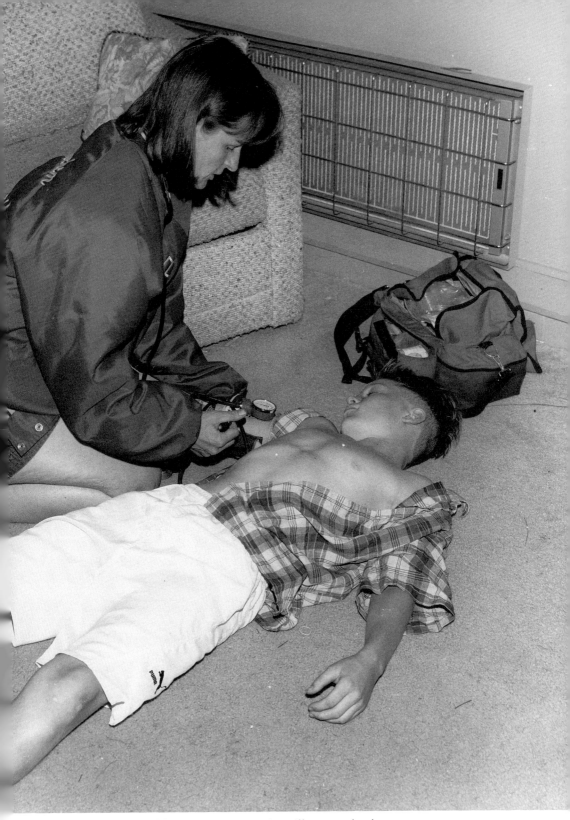

An overdose of drugs can cause serious illness or death.

40

into which they inject the drug burns immediately afterward.

- Regular use of China White causes severe, painful constipation. Because of that it is sometimes cut with a mild laxative.
- Users of China White report that it causes their muscles to become painfully hard and rigid.
- China White causes low blood pressure, which presents the danger of heart failure and possible death.
- Users develop uncontrollable shaking of the arms, legs, and head. This condition is *permanent*.
- Respiratory depression, or sloweddown breathing, affects users of China White. As the rate of breathing slows, the level of oxygen in the blood becomes dangerously low, damaging the body's cells.
- Many users of China White become paralyzed *permanently*. They will spend the rest of their lives in a hospital or nursing home.
- Users of China White may die because of overdosing. The overdose may be accidental, or it may occur because the drug was cut with another drug that intensified its effect.

All of these physical problems are possible every time you use this drug. Many people have experienced them after only one use. Think about it—is the rush really worth the risk?

MPPP

MPPP is another drug that was designed to replace heroin. It is sometimes called the "new heroin."

Making MPPP is very difficult. Many chemicals must be cooked together for a long time—about 10 hours. The temperature must remain constantly at 30° Celsius. Over 40° the drug becomes a poison.

This poison that results is called MPTP. When MPTP is injected into the body, it is very dangerous because it goes directly to the brain. There it kills certain cells that are responsible for movement.

These are the symptoms of MPTP :

1. When the drug is injected into a vein, it burns severely.
2. The arms, legs, and head begin to twitch or jerk.
3. The muscles begin to tighten up. They feel very sore.
4. The muscles begin to freeze in place so that the addict can barely move.

42

5. The whole body freezes in place. The only functions left are breathing, hearing, and thinking.

6. The eyelids won't open; the person might as well be blind.

Remember, many of these people had never used drugs before.

Remember also that they couldn't tell that their drug was poison. But it cripples and kills the people who use it.

There is only one way to be safe: don't use drugs!

Ice

Ephedrine is a drug that was used by the ancient Chinese as medicine in herb tea.

In the 1920s the drug amphetamine, which acted like ephedrine, was manufactured. It was used to treat narcolepsy, or sleeping sickness. Those who used it found that they could stay awake for long periods of time. They also discovered that they were able to do almost everything faster.

Soon college students began experimenting with amphetamine. They often used it to help them stay awake to cram for exams. Truck drivers used it to help them stay awake during long trips. In

Students sometimes try drugs to increase their energy for studying.

World War II the United States military used the drug during long battles. By the 1950s doctors were using it to treat fatigue and depression.

Ice is a drug that was designed to replace amphetamine. It is many times more addictive than crack. That makes it the most addictive drug in the world.

People who use ice experience a rush similar to the one they get from crack. It is much more intense, however. It also lasts much longer. One dose causes the user to stay awake for several days.

44

Like crack, ice is smoked. However, one dosage can be smoked many times. That makes it less expensive to use. People may stay awake for weeks at a time on just one dosage.

Users of ice may experience dizziness, anxiety, rapid heart beat, increased blood pressure, heart attack, and stroke. In some cases paranoia, delusions, and hallucinations occur.

At the present time, ice has been reported only on the West Coast. It is possible, however, that the drug will make its way into other parts of the United States.

Angel Dust

Angel dust was first developed as a tranquilizer for large animals. Doctors of veterinary medicine (vets) used it to keep animals asleep during surgery. It is so powerful that it was used on elephants.

The street names for angel dust include PCP, dust, rocket fuel, Special K, magic, and cyclone.

People who use the drug hallucinate—they see, hear, or smell things that aren't really there. Sometimes this is pleasant ("a good trip"). Other times it can be frightening and dangerous ("a bad trip").

Bad trips are sometimes fatal. People may imagine that they are being attacked by an animal or insects. When this happens, they begin fighting or running. They may injure a friend or someone they don't even know trying to get away from whatever they believe is after them. They may try to escape by jumping out of a window, even if it's several stories high.

Because people using PCP feel no pain, it is very difficult to restrain them. People

45

A drug user's behavior may be dangerous and uncontrollable.

46 have been known to keep fighting or running even after they have been shot or lost an arm.

One of the worst things about angel dust is that users may have "flashbacks." A flashback is experiencing a trip some time after having stopped using the drug. It can happen even years later.

Crank

Crank is a drug that was designed to replace cocaine. Crank is much like cocaine. But most people can tell the difference.

It is usually cut with a white powder. Sometimes the sugars sucrose, fructose, or lactose are used. Other powders used are cornstarch, baking soda, or arsenic (an insecticide or weed killer).

The chemical name for crank is methaphetamine. It is sometimes used in medicine to treat sleeping sickness.

Street names for crank include meth, crystal, glass, and go-fast. The most common name is speed. That is because it makes users do everything at a faster pace. They walk faster, work faster, talk faster, and stay awake longer.

Crank can be snorted, put into capsules and swallowed, or mainlined. The rush is most powerful when it is mainlined.

Crank produces a rush that is very strong and may last up to six hours. Those who use it feel very smart. They feel that they can do almost anything. They believe that all of their problems are gone.

When the drug wears off, the users come down quickly. They become very depressed, so they use more crank.

Some people do this over and over. They call it a "run." Runs can last for weeks. When a run is over, the depression is terrible. Users are so tired that they may sleep for days. Coming down off a run is called "crashing."

The use of crank has many side effects. Among the psychological effects, users have a hard time looking others in the eye when speaking. They can become violent for little or no reason. They may also experience depression, confusion, anger, forgetfulness, and paranoia.

Among physical effects, users often have a dry mouth, enlarged pupils, a run-down feeling, and a runny nose (if they snort the drug). They may be unable to stop sticking the tongue out. They may have frequent headaches or muscle twitching. More serious effects are low tolerance to sickness, brain damage, convulsions, heart attack, stroke, and death.

The desire to be accepted, or the attempt to escape problems, are two common reasons for becoming involved with drugs.

CHAPTER 4

Why People Use Drugs

It is important for you to understand why people use drugs. No one ever starts out to become addicted. People use drugs for very specific reasons.

To Be Popular

Everyone wants to be popular. We all want other people to like us. That's normal. But some people are afraid that if they refuse drugs others won't like them.

It might seem as if all the best kids are doing drugs. That is not true. If you really look around your school or neighborhood, you will discover that the nicest kids are the ones who *don't* use drugs.

Remember, the "druggies" get to the point where they will do anything for

50 drugs. They will use you. They will turn their back on you. All for drugs. Why would you want them for friends?

To Fight Boredom
Lots of kids use drugs because they are bored. They think that nothing is going on in their lives.

Well, using drugs does solve that problem. Soon, nothing *but* drugs is going on in their lives. They need to use at school: What if they get caught? They need to use at home: What if their parents find out? They need more drugs: Where will they get the money?

What would have happened if these kids had put that much time and energy into something else? A sport? Their studies? Girls? Boys? Friends? Family? A hobby? Wouldn't that be a better way to handle your feeling of boredom?

To Deal with Problems
Lots of kids use drugs to deal with problems. They get kicked off the team—they use drugs. Their parents divorce—they use drugs. They break up with a boyfriend or girlfriend—they use drugs. Whatever the problem, they use drugs. Of course, what they end up with is more problems.

Using drugs doesn't make problems go away. It just hides them for a while. Then all the problems are still there plus another one: addiction!

Is this what you want for yourself? Remember, this problem is bigger than any other problems you may have had. It can destroy your life.

Wouldn't it be better to deal with the problem *without the drugs?*

To Keep Others from Thinking They Are Chicken

Imagine people taking drugs because they are afraid. Well, it really proves they *are* afraid!

It takes courage to resist drugs. Only cowards worry about and act according to what others think. Taking drugs just proves that you are *not* smart.

To Make Life Seem Less Awful

These are the truly unfortunate kids. Their lives are so miserable that taking drugs makes them seem better. But actually, drugs make things worse.

Drugs only work for a little while. Then you have to take more. Pretty soon you are taking larger amounts of the drug to get a rush.

52   Why keep doing that when you could spend the same amount of time and money making yourself happy?

To Get Revenge

Some kids use drugs because they have been hurt by someone. They want to make that person feel hurt, too.

Does that make sense? Something is a little crazy when people hurt themselves to get even.

Remember, the other person may not even know that you are trying to hurt him or her. He or she won't know, and you'll be hooked on drugs. So who is really hurt?

To Satisfy an Addiction

Once people begin using drugs, they become addicted quickly. They need the drug to keep going. They need the drug to prevent withdrawal. Withdrawal can be extremely painful. Addicts fear being without drugs more than anything.

If that were not true, why would they use drugs? Every designer drug and many of the other drugs could kill the user. Why would someone take a chance on dying? Because he or she is addicted.

CHAPTER 5

Where to Get Help

If you've read the first part of this book, it probably scared you. If you, a friend, or a family member have been doing drugs, you may be asking, "Where can I go for help?" Actually, there are several places.

Your Parents

Of course, your first reaction to that is, "You've got to be crazy! They'd kill me." Not true.

Believe it or not, your parents can be the best supporting factor if you sincerely want to get off drugs. You may even be surprised. You may find out that your parents know a lot about drugs. They may know from research such as reading books

54 and articles, attending lectures on the subject, or watching television programs. Or they may even have had drug problems when they were growing up.

The biggest problem will be overcoming your fear—the fear of having to tell them that you are on drugs. Just trying to find the right words is hard. Sometimes getting their attention is even harder. You can always leave pamphlets about drugs in a place where they will find them. You can get a book and ask them to read it. But, you *will* need to tell them.

You fear their reaction. Don't let your mind dream up all the horrible things that can happen. Don't torture yourself. That will only add to your fear. You are going through enough already. You have no way of knowing how your parents will react until you tell them.

You fear what they will make you do. Your parents won't make you do anything worse than what you've already done to yourself. You may also be concerned that, because of your parents' own problems, they can't give you the support that you need. You might feel bad about adding to their grief.

These are all valid fears. But try to remember that your parents love you and

Talking to parents or friends may help with seeing problems
more clearly and avoiding drugs as a solution.

56 care about you. You will find that they will go to great lengths to help you with your drug problem, despite what they are going through themselves.

Minister, Priest, or Rabbi

Many members of the clergy have been trained to help kids with drug problems. They often know a good deal about drugs and addiction. They may be able to help you find a counselor.

They may also be able to help you tell your parents, if you can't. Remember, most people who enter the clergy do so because they want to help people. All you need to do to get their help is to ask for it.

If you don't have a priest, minister, or rabbi, with whom you can talk, make use of a drug-abuse hotline.

The Drug-Abuse Hotline

Many cities have drug-abuse hotlines. The phones are answered by people who know how to help you. You don't have to give your name.

If you don't have a drug-abuse hotline in your city, you may have another kind of hotline. Try "Contact" or "Teen Line." If you can't find one, don't give up. Many people want to help you.

Your Teacher

Often teachers turn out to be really great helpers for kids on drugs. Your job is, of course, to tell your teacher about your problem. Ask if you could talk to him or her after class.

School Counselor

If you aren't able to tell your teacher, go to your school counselors. All of them are trained to help kids. Some of them are specifically trained to deal with kids on drugs.

Tell your teacher you want to see a school counselor. Your teacher may make an appointment for you. Or you can make one yourself.

If your school doesn't have counselors, or if it is summer break from school, keep on reading.

Self-Help Groups

There are many kinds of self-help groups. Some of them are Alcoholics Anonymous (AA), Narcotics Anonymous (NA), Cocaine Anonymous (CA), Alateen, and Al-Anon. They are listed in the white pages of your telephone directory.

People there are usually very helpful. Most of them are former addicts or have a

58 family member who is an addict. They have experienced addiction first-hand. Because of this, they want to help.

If you can't find a self-help group, don't quit trying.

Alcohol and Drug Counselor

Look in the yellow pages of your telephone directory to find one of these specialists. They may be listed in several ways. Try looking under the following headings: Alcohol Counselors, Drug Counselors, Drug and Alcohol Counselors, Alcohol and Drug Counselors, Drug Treatment Centers, Hospitals, Chemical Dependency Counselors, or Addiction Specialists.

If you want help badly enough, you will be able to tell one of these people about your drug use and ask for help.

Conclusion

As you know by now, designer drugs are a big problem in our society. The only way we can deal with a problem so big is to get involved.

Now that you have read this book, it is time to ask yourself this question, "So what can I do?" There are several things you can do!

- DON'T experiment with drugs. Remember, some of them can make you
  addicted after the first time.
- DON'T let your friends, family, or
  other adults talk you into experimenting with drugs.
- If you have already tried drugs,
  DON'T use them again.
- If you can't stop, or just don't want to
  stop, get help immediately.
- If you know someone who is using
  drugs, report it. You could save a life.
- If you know someone who is selling
  drugs, report it. But *be careful*. Dealers may try to hurt you if you tell on
  them.
- Tell your friends and family members
  not to use drugs. Tell them how dangerous they are.
- If your school, church, or synagogue
  has a drug awareness group or pro-
  gram, get involved. Get your family
  and friends involved, too.

If you do these things, you can make a
difference. There is a way to win the
battle against drugs, and it starts with you
and me.

Help List

Telephone Book (Yellow Pages)
- Drug Abuse, Alcoholism, Counselors

Associations
- American Council for Drug Education
  204 Monroe Street
  Rockville, MD 20852
  (301) 294-0600

- Narcotics Anonymous
  World Service Office
  16155 Wyandotte Street
  Van Nuys, CA 91406
  (818) 780-3951

- Al-Anon / Alateen Headquarters
  P.O. Box 862, Midtown Station
  New York, NY 10018
  (800) 356-9996

Call Toll-Free
- The Cocaine Hotline
  (800)-COCAINE

- National Institute on Drug Abuse
  (800) 662-HELP

- Drug and Alcohol Hotline
  (800) 252-6465

Glossary
Explaining New Words

addiction Inability to stop using a particular substance, usually a drug.

anhedonia Inability to feel pleasure.

genetic code Chemical instructions that cause the body to react in certain ways.

hallucination Experience of something that does not exist; seeing, hearing, or smelling things that are not present.

paranoia Mental illness in which a person believes that most other people intend to hurt him or her.

psychedelic Drug that causes the user to experience intense images or sounds.

psychosis Mental illness in which a person loses touch with the real world.

quality control In manufacturing, a system for insuring that each item produced is of the same level of quality.

schizophrenia Mental illness that causes delusions and difficulty in speech and behavior.

suppressor Substance that can prevent the normal action of another substance.

tolerance Ability to endure or resist the effects of a substance, such as a drug.

tranquilizer In medicine, a drug that has a calming, relaxing effect.

For Further Reading

Ball, Jacqueline. *Everything You Need to Know about Drug Abuse*, rev. ed. New York: The Rosen Publishing Group, 1992.

Clayton, Lawrence. *Coping with a Drug-Abusing Parent*. New York: The Rosen Publishing Group, 1991.

Edwards, Gabrielle. *Coping with Drug Abuse*, rev. ed. New York: The Rosen Publishing Group, 1990.

Jackson, Michael and Brude. *Doing Drugs*. New York: St. Martin's, 1983.

Kaplan, Leslie. *Coping with Peer Pressure*, rev. ed. New York: The Rosen Publishing Group, 1993.

Lee, Essie. *Breaking the Connection*. New York: Messner, 1988.

Mothner, Ira, and Weitz, Alan. *How to Get Off Drugs*. New York: Rolling Stone Press, 1985.

Smith, Sandra Lee. *Coping with Decision Making*, rev. ed. New York: The Rosen Publishing Group, 1994.

_____. *Value of Self-Control*. New York: The Rosen Publishing Group, 1991.

Sunshine, Linda, and Wright, John. *The 100 Best Treatment Centers for Alcoholism and Drug Abuse*. New York: Avon, 1988.

Index

A
addiction, 16, 17, 23, 33, 34,
    37, 38, 52, 58
addicts, 22, 32, 58
amphetamine, 27, 42–43
    World War II and, 43
angel dust, 12, 43, 44, 45–46
anhedonia, 12, 23
anxiety, 12, 27, 44

B
bad trips, 44
baking soda, 27
burning-arm syndrome, 38

C
caffeine, 27, 31
China White, 12, 34, 35–38,
    40–41
cocaine, 28, 30–31, 33, 46
cook joints, 9
cooks, 9, 10, 12
crack, 13, 15–16, 22–23, 28,
    31, 33
crack houses, 9, 33
crank, 46–47
cut, 11, 34, 36

D
dealers, 19, 21–22, 33, 35, 37
depression, 12, 23, 27, 47
designer drugs
    how to get, 15–16, 18–23
    kinds of, 25–28, 30–31,
        33–38
    psychological effects of,
        11, 23, 27
    what are, 9–13

E
Ectasy, 25–27
endorphin, 16
ephedrine, 42

F
flashbacks, 46
freebase, 31

G
genetic code, 16, 18

H
hallucinations, 12, 44
heart attack, 10, 27, 44, 47
help, where to get, 53–54,
    56–59
heroin, 22, 34–35, 36, 37, 38
high-addictive potential, 38
hotlines, 56

I
ice, 42, 43–44
insomnia, 10, 23

L
laboratories, 9, 10, 35–36,
lace, 37
lactose, 36, 46
laxative, 31, 40
lung disease, 10, 23

M
mainline, 30
mannitol, 36
marijuana, 18
MDMA (see ecstasy)
methaphetamine, 46 (see
    also crank)
moon rock, 22
morphine, 34, 36
    Civil War and, 34
MPPP, 41
MPTP, 36, 41–42

N
nausea, 10, 23, 27
nosebleeds, 10, 23

63

64

O
overdosing, 40

P
paralysis, 10
paranoia, 11, 12, 27, 44, 47
Parkinson's disease, 10
PCP (*see* angel dust)
peer pressure, 18, 19
peyote, 25–26, 27
psychosis, 11

R
rock cocaine, 31 (*see also* crack)

S
schizophrenia, 23
self-help groups, 57
skin-popping, 37

snort, 28, 37
social withdrawal, 12, 23
speed, 27, 31 (*see also* amphetamine)
spitting up blood, 11
stomach problems, 10
stroke, 10, 23, 27, 44, 47
strychnine, 36
sucrose, 46
sugar, 27, 31

T
talculm powder, 31
THIQ, 16

V
vomiting, 10, 23, 27

W
withdrawal, 52

About the Author
Dr. Lawrence Clayton earned his doctorate from Texas Woman's University. He is an ordained minister and has served as such since 1972. Dr. Clayton is a clinical marriage and family therapist and certified drug and alcohol counselor. He is also president of the Oklahoma Professional Drug and Alcohol Counselor's Certification Board. Dr. Clayton lives with his wife, Cathy, and their three children in Piedmont, Oklahoma.

Photo Credits
Cover: Gamma-Liaison.
Pages 2, 45: Wide World Photos; pp. 8, 14, 17, 20, 24, 32, 39, 43, 48, 55: Stuart Rabinowitz; p. 30 © Georges Merillon/ Gamma-Liaison; p. 35: Gamma-Liaison.

Design & Production: Blackbirch Graphics, Inc.